ART
A WORLD OF WORDS

First Paintings — First Words in 12 Languages

Doris Kutschbach

ART A WORLD OF WORDS

First Paintings — First Words in 12 Languages

PRESTEL
Munich · London · New York

Dear parents,

People use art and language to communicate with one another, and children should begin exploring both at a young age.

Young children see art with different eyes than we do. They are not interested in who painted a picture or why. They look at paintings with fresh eyes—searching for what is familiar or exciting to them. Children also use their earliest language to describe what they experience every day. Their first words represent the people and things around them (father or dog) or the activities they do (play, eat, or sleep). As they explore more of the world, children begin learning the words for things they've discovered: parts of their bodies; new spaces and places; animals, plants, and seasons.

In this book, we present artworks from several countries that depict subjects familiar or interesting to children. Next to each picture are appropriate first words in twelve diffe-rent languages—with phonetic pronunciations for reading the words aloud. This format helps children begin to learn their own language and the language of other cultures. It also makes them more sensitive to the colorful, vibrant creations of art.

Together, you and your children can use this book to explore a world of sounds and images.

Doris Kutschbach

The languages in this book:

Arabic	French	Hebrew	Korean
Chinese	German	Italian	Russian
English	Greek	Japanese	Spanish

Familie
[faˈmiːli̯ə]

가족
[ka.ɹok]

family
[fæmɪlɪ]

家庭
[jiātíng]

famille
[famij]

أسرة
[ˈʔusrə]

familia
[faˈmilja]

משפחה
[miʃpaˈħa]

famiglia
[faˈmiʎʎɐ]

かぞく
[kadzokɯ]

οικογένεια
[ikɔˈjɛnia]

семья
[sʲɪmʲˈjæ]

Edgar Degas, *The Bellelli Family*

mother	**Mama**
[ˈmʌðəʳ]	[ˈmama]
maman	**엄마**
[mamɑ̃]	[əm.ma]
mamá	**妈妈**
[maˈma]	[māma]
mamma	**لٵلٵ**
[ˈmamma]	[ˈmæːmæː]
μαμά	**אימא**
[maˈma]	[ˈima]
Мама	**おかあさん**
[ˈmamə]	[okaːsan]

Tsugouharu Foujita, *The Children of Akita*

papa

[papa]

papá

[pa'pa]

papà

[pa'pa]

μπαμπάς

[ba'bas]

папа

['papə]

おとうさん

[oto:san]

father

['fa:ðəʳ]

Papa

['papa]

아빠

[a.p'a]

爸爸

[bàba]

بابا

['bæ:bæ:]

אבא

['aba]

Francks Deceus, *Father and Child*

niños
['niɲos]

enfants
[ãfã]

bambini
[bamˈbiːni]

children
[ˈtʃɪldrən]

παιδιά
[pɛˈðja]

Kinder
[ˈkɪndɐ]

дети
[ˈdʲetʲɪ]

아이들
[a.i.tɨːl]

こども
[kodomo]

孩子
[háizi]

ילדים
[jelaˈdim]

أطفال
[ˈʔatˤfæːl]

Tadeusz Makowski, *At the Cradle*

neonato

[neo'na:to]

μωρό

[mɔ'rɔ]

ребенок

[rʲɪ'bʲɵnək]

あかちゃん

[akatʃan]

תינוק

[ti'nok]

رضيع

[ra'dˤiːʕ]

bebé

[be'βe]

bébé

[bebe]

baby

['beɪbɪ]

Baby

['be:bi]

아기

[a.gi]

婴儿

[yīng'ér]

Bernardo Strozzi, *Sleeping Child*

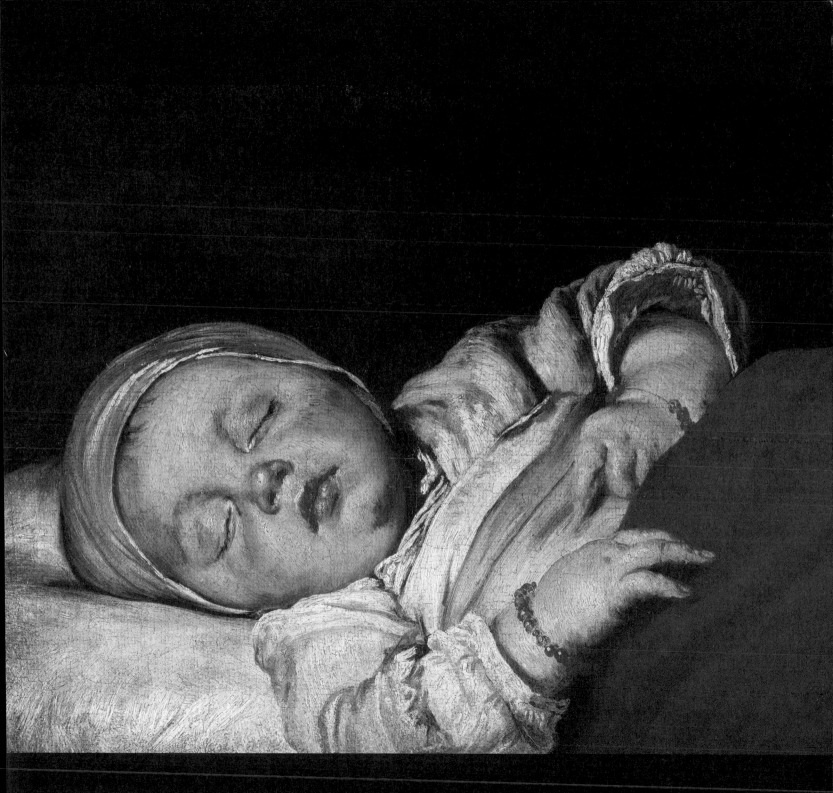

μάτι
['mati]

occhio
['ɔkkio]

глаз
[glas]

ojo
['oxo]

め
[me]

oeil
[oej]

עין
['ʕajin]

eye
[aɪ]

عين
[ʕʌjn]

Auge
['aʊ̯ɡə]

眼睛
[yǎnjīng]

눈
[nun]

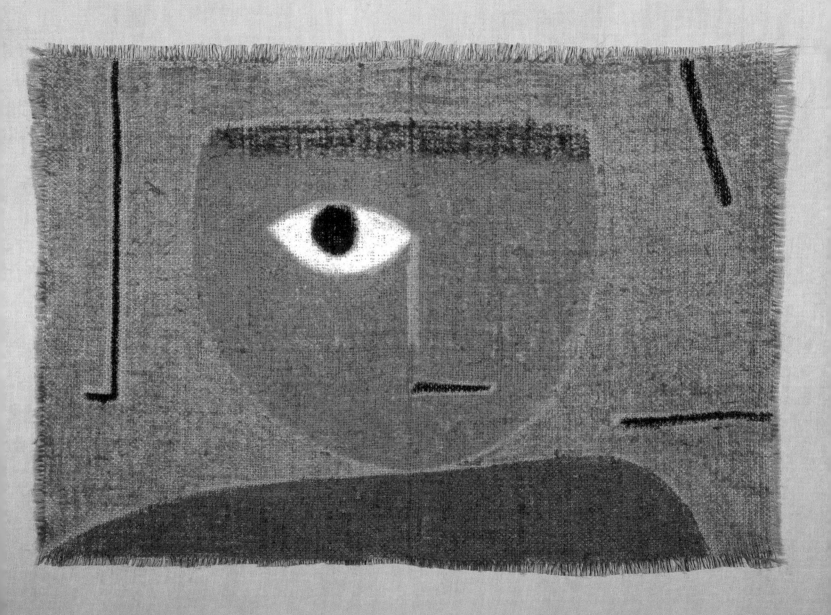

HOC
[nos]

はな
[hana]

אף
[af]

أنف
[ʔænf]

鼻子
[bízi]

코
[kʰo]

μύτη
['miti]

naso
['na:zo]

nariz
[na'riθ]

nez
[ne]

nose
[nəʊz]

Nase
['na:zə]

Edward Lear, Illustration from *A Book of Nonsense*

くち
[kɯtʃi]

рот
[rot]

פה
[pe]

στόμα
['stɔma]

فم
[fæm]

bocca
['bokka]

嘴巴
[zuǐba]

boca
['boka]

입
[ip]

bouche
[buʃ]

Mund
['mʊnt]

mouth
[maʊθ]

Salvador Dalí, *Mae West Lips Sofa*

אוֹזֶן
['ozen]

みみ
[mimi]

أُذُن
[ʔuðun]

ухо
['uxə]

耳朵
[ěrduō]

αυτί
[af'ti]

귀
[kwi]

orecchio
[o'rekkio]

Ohr
['oːɐ̯]

oreja
[o'rexa]

ear
[ɪə]

oreille
[ɔʀɛj]

Unknown artist, *Bust of the Roman Emperor Caracalla*

شَعر

[ʃʌʕɾ]

שׂיעָר

[seˈʕaʁ]

头发

[tóufa]

かみ

[kami]

머리카락

[mə.ri.kʰa.rak]

волосы

[ˈvoləsɨ]

Haare

[haːrə]

μαλλιά

[maˈʎa]

hair

[hɛə]

capelli

[kaˈpelli]

cheveux

[ʃəvø]

cabello

[kaˈβeʎo]

Edgar Degas, *Woman at Her Toilette*

手
[shǒu]

ﻳﺪﺍﻥ
[jæˈdæːn]

손
[son]

ידיים
[jaˈdajim]

Hände
[ˈhɛndə]

て
[te]

hands
[hændz]

руки
[ˈrukʲɪ]

mains
[mɛ̃]

mani
[ˈmaːni]

manos
[ˈmãnos]

χέρια
[ˈçɛria]

Michelangelo Buonarroti, *The Creation of Adam*

늙다
[nɨl.t'a]

老
[lǎo]

alt
[alt]

شيخة
[ʃæjxə]

old
[əʊld]

זקנה
[zke'na]

vieux
[vjø]

おとしより
[otoʃiyori]

vieja
['bjexa]

старый
['starɨj]

anziana
[an'tsia:na]

ηλικιωμένη
[iliciɔ'mɛni]

Albrecht Dürer, *The Artist's Mother*

fröhlich
['fʁøːlɪç]

happy
['hæpɪ]

joyeux
[ʒwajø]

alegre
[a'leɣre]

allegro
[al'legro]

χαρούμενος
[xa'rumɛnɔs]

즐겁다
[cil.gəp.t'a]

欢乐
[huānlè]

فرحان
[far'ħæːn]

שׂמח
[sa'meaħ]

たのしい
[tanoʃiː]

веселый
[vʲɪ'sʲɵlɨj]

Odilon Redon, *Smiling Spider*

sad

[sæd]

triste

[tʀɪst]

triste

[ˈtɾiʂte]

tristi

[ˈtɾisti]

λυπημένος

[lipiˈmɛnɔs]

грустный

[ˈgrusnɨj]

traurig

[ˈtʀaʊ̯ʀɪç]

슬프다

[sɯl.pʰɨ.da]

悲伤

[bēishāng]

حزين

[ħæˈziːn]

עצוב

[ʕaˈt͡suv]

かなしい

[kanaɕiː]

Unknown Spanish artist, *Mourners*

피곤하다
[pʰi.gon.ha.da]

κουρασμένος
[kuraz'mɛnɔs]

müde
['myːdə]

усталый
[ʊsˈtalɪj]

tired
['taɪəd]

ねむい
[nemɯi]

fatigué
[fatige]

עייף
[ʕaˈjef]

cansado
[kanˈsaðo]

تعبان
[tʌʕˈbæːn]

stanco
['staŋko]

累
[lèi]

متوحش
[mutæˈwæħħiʃ]

sauvage
[sovaʒ]

wild
[waɪld]

野蛮
[yěmán]

ワイルド
[wairɯdo]

salvaje
[salˈβaxe]

selvaggio
[selˈvaddʒo]

פרא
[ˈpeʁe]

야생적이다
[ja.səŋ.cək.i.da]

wild
[vɪlt]

άγριος
[ˈaɣriɔs]

дикий
[ˈdʲikʲɪj]

Dogon Leopard Mask, Mali

manger

[mɑ̃ʒe]

to eat

[tə iːt]

comer

[koˈmer]

essen

[ˈɛsn̩]

mangiare

[manˈdʒaːre]

먹다

[mək.tʼa]

τρώω

[ˈtrɔɔ]

吃

[chī]

есть

[jesʲtʲ]

أكل

[ʔækl]

たべる

[tabeɾɯ]

לאכול

[leeˈχol]

Carl Larsson, *The Evening Meal*

dormir

[dɔʀmiʀ]

to sleep

[tə sliːp]

schlafen

[ˈʃlaːfn̩]

dormir

[dorˈmir]

dormire

[dorˈmiːre]

κοιμάμαι

[ciˈmamɛ]

睡

[shuì]

نوم

[næwm]

자다

[ca.da]

לישון

[liˈʃon]

ねむる

[nemɯɾɯ]

спать

[spatʲ]

玩

[wán]

놀다

[no:l.da]

لعب

[lʌʕb]

לשחק

[lesaˈħek]

играть

[ɪgˈratʲ]

あそぶ

[asobɯ]

jouer

[ʒwe]

παίζω

[ˈpɛzɔ]

to play

[tə pleɪ]

giocare

[dʒoˈka:re]

spielen

[ˈʃpi:lən]

jugar

[xuˈɣar]

Mary Cassatt, *Children on the Beach*

그네를 타다
[kɨ.ne.rɨl.tʰa.da]

schaukeln
[ˈʃaʊ̯kl̩n]

荡秋千
[dàngqiūqiān]

to swing
[tə swɪŋ]

تَأَرْجَحَ
[ˈtæˈʔardʒuħ]

se balancer
[sə balɑ̃se]

להתנדנד
[leħitnadˈned]

columpiar
[kolumˈpjar]

ゆれる
[jɯɾeɾɯ]

andare in altalena
[anˈdaːre in altaˈleːna]

качаться
[kɐˈtɕætsə]

κάνω κούνια
[ˈkanɔ ˈkuɲa]

Jean-Honoré Fragonard, *The Swing*

춤추다

[cʰum.cʰu.da]

danser

[dɑ̃se]

χορεύω

[xɔˈrɛvɔ]

跳舞

[tiàowǔ]

おどる

[odoɾɯ]

bailar

[bai̯ˈlar]

ballare

[balˈlaːre]

رقص

[raqsˤ]

танцевать

[tənt͡sɕeˈvatʲ]

לרקוד

[liʁˈkod]

tanzen

[ˈtantsn̩]

to dance

[tə dɑːns]

Ernst Ludwig Kirchner, *Russian Dancer*

correr
[koˈřer]

courir
[kuʀiʀ]

correre
[ˈkorrere]

to run
[tə rʌn]

τρέχω
[ˈtrɛxɔ]

laufen
[ˈlaʊ̯fn̩]

бежать
[bʲɪˈʐatʲ]

달리다
[tal.li.da]

はしる
[haʃiɾɯ]

跑
[pǎo]

לרוץ
[laˈʁut͡s]

ركض
[rakdˤ]

Unknown Greek artist, *Race*

להתקלח

[leħitka'leaħ]

bañar

[ba'ɲar]

bath time

[beɪð taɪm]

baden

['ba:dn̩]

목욕하다

[mok.jok.ha.da]

洗澡

[xǐzǎo]

おふろ

[oɸɯro]

купаться

[kʊ'patsə]

fare il bagno

['fa:re il 'baɲno]

κάνω μπάνιο

['kanɔ 'baɲɔ]

استحمام

[istiħ'ma:m]

prendre un bain

[pʀɑ̃dʀ œ̃ bɛ̃]

Henri Lebasque, *The Bath*

piangere
['piandʒere]

llorar
[ʎoˈrar]

κλαίω
[ˈklɛɔ]

pleurer
[ploeʁe]

плакать
[ˈplakətʲ]

to cry
[tə kraɪ]

なく
[nakɯ]

weinen
[ˈvaɪ̯nən]

לבכות
[liv̥ˈkot]

울다
[ul.da]

تَبْكِي
[tabˈkiː]

哭
[kū]

Roy Lichtenstein, *Crying Girl*

φιλώ

[fiˈlɔ]

целовать

[t͡səleˈvatʲ]

キス

[kisɯ]

לנשק

[lenaˈʃek]

تقبيل

[taqˈbiːl]

吻

[wěn]

baciare

[baˈt͡ʃaːre]

besar

[beˈsar]

embrasser

[ɑ̃bʁase]

to kiss

[tə kɪs]

küssen

[ˈkʏsn̩]

뽀뽀하다

[pʼo.pʼo.ha.da]

Mary Cassatt, *A Goodnight Kiss*

chambre
[ʃɑ̃bʀ]

camera
[ˈkaːmera]

방
[paŋ]

δωμάτιο
[ðɔˈmatiɔ]

房间
[fángjiān]

комната
[ˈkomnətə]

غرفة
[ˈɣurfə]

habitación
[aβitaˈθjon]

חדר
[ˈħedeʁ]

room
[ruːm]

へや
[heja]

Zimmer
[ˈtsɪmɐ]

Vincent van Gogh, *Bedroom in Arles*

кухня
['kuxnʲə]

Küche
['kʏçə]

だいどころ
[daidokoɾo]

kitchen
['kɪtʃɪn]

מטבח
[mitˈbaħ]

cuisine
[kɥizin]

مطبخ
['matˤbæx]

cocina
[koˈθina]

厨房
[chúfáng]

cucina
[kuˈtʃiːna]

부엌
[pu.ək]

κουζίνα
[kuˈzina]

Adolf Heinrich Hansen, *A Woman Reading in an Interior*

いえ
[ie]

ДОМ
[dom]

בית
['bajit]

σπίτι
['spiti]

بيت
[bæjt]

casa
['ka:za]

房子
[fángzi]

casa
['kasa]

집
[cip]

maison
[mɛz�õ]

Haus
[haʊs]

house
[haʊs]

Wilhelm Morgner, *Brick Baker*

אַרְמוֹן

[aʁˈmon]

おしろ

[oʃiɾo]

замок

[ˈzamək]

πύργος

[ˈpirɣɔs]

castello

[kasˈtɛllo]

castillo

[kasˈtiʎo]

Schloss

[ʃlɔs]

castle

[ˈkɑːsəl]

château

[ʃɑto]

성

[səŋ]

宮殿

[gōngdiàn]

قصر

[qasˤr]

Limbourg Brothers, *The Month September*

حديقة
[ħæˈdiːqa]

花园
[huāyuán]

정원
[cəŋ.wən]

Garten
[ˈɡaʁtn̩]

garden
[ˈɡɑːdən]

jardin
[ʒaʁdɛ̃]

jardín
[xarˈðin]

giardino
[dʒarˈdiːno]

κήπος
[ˈcipɔs]

сад
[sat]

にわ
[niwa]

גינה
[giˈna]

August Macke, *Children in the Garden*

市场
[shìchǎng]

mercato
[merˈkaːto]

سوق
[suːq]

mercado
[merˈkaðo]

שוק
[ʃuk]

marché
[maʁʃe]

いちば
[itʃiba]

market
[ˈmɑːkɪt]

рынок
[ˈrɨnək]

Markt
[maʁkt]

αγορά
[aɣɔˈra]

시장
[ʃiːʤaŋ]

Félix Vallotton, *At the Market*

ПЛЯЖ

[plʲæʂ]

はまべ

[hamabe]

חוף

[ħof]

شاطئ

[ˈʃaːtˤiʔ]

沙滩

[shātān]

바닷가

[pa.da(t).kʼa]

παραλία

[paraˈlia]

spiaggia

[ˈspiaddʒa]

playa

[ˈplaǰa]

plage

[plaʒ]

beach

[biːtʃ]

Strand

[ʃtʀant]

Edward Henry Potthast, *Beach Life*

まち
[matʃi]

город
['gorət]

עיר
[ʕiʁ]

πόλη
['pɔli]

مدينة
[mæ'diːnə]

città
[tʃit'ta]

城市
[chéngshì]

ciudad
[θju'ðað]

도시
[to.ʃi]

ville
[vil]

Stadt
[ʃtat]

city
['sɪtɪ]

Paul Cornoyer, *Urban Nocturne*

숲
[sup]

Wald
[valt]

森林
[sēnlín]

forest
['fɒrɪst]

غابة
['ɣʌːbə]

forêt
[fɔʀɛ]

יער
['jaʃaʁ]

bosque
['boske]

もり
[moɾi]

bosco
['bɔsko]

лес
[lʲes]

δάσος
['ðasɔs]

Paul Gauguin, *Landscape with Blue Tree Trunks*

Urwald
[ˈuːɐ̯ˌvalt]

원시림
[wən.si.rim]

jungle
[ˈdʒʌŋɡəl]

ג'ונגל
[ˈd͡ʒuŋɡel]

selva
[ˈselβa]

げんしりん
[genʃiɾin]

giungla
[ˈdʒuŋɡla]

джунгли
[ˈdʐunɡlʲɪ]

原始森林
[yuánshǐsēnlín]

παρθένο δάσος
[parˈθɛnɔ ˈðasɔs]

أَدغال
[ʔædˈɣaːl]

jungle
[ʒɑ̃ɡl]

зоопарк

[zɐɐ'park]

גן חיות

[gan ħaˈjot]

ZOO

[ˈθoo]

zoo

[zuː]

动物园

[dòngwùyuán]

zoo

[zo]

ζωολογικός κήπος

[zɔɔlɔjiˈkɔs ˈcipɔs]

ZOO

[ˈdzɔːo]

동물원

[toŋ.mul.wən]

Zoo

[tsoː]

حديقة الحيوانات

[ħæˈdiːqat æl-ħæjæwæːˈnæːt]

どうぶつえん

[doːbɯtsɯen]

August Macke, *Large Zoological Garden*

马戏团

[mǎxìtuán]

서커스

[sʼə.kʰə.sɨ]

Zirkus

[ˈtsɪʁkʊs]

circus

[ˈsɜːkəs]

cirque

[sɪʁk]

circo

[ˈθirko]

سيرك

[sirk]

קרקס

[kiʁˈkas]

サーカス

[saːkasɯ]

цирк

[t͡sɨrk]

τσίρκο

[ˈtsirkɔ]

circo

[ˈtʃirko]

농장
[noŋ.ʨaŋ]

农场
[nóngchǎng]

Bauernhof
[ˈbaʊ̯n̩ˌhoːf]

مزرعة
[ˈmæzraʕʌ]

farm
[fɑːm]

חווה
[ħaˈva]

ferme
[fɛʀm]

のうじょう
[noːdʑoː]

granja
[ˈgraŋxa]

ферма
[ˈfʲermə]

fattoria
[fattoˈriːa]

αγρόκτημα
[aˈɣɾɔktima]

Unknown American artist, *Landscape with Figures*

Kuh

[ku:]

cow

[kaʊ]

vache

[vaʃ]

vaca

[ˈbaka]

mucca

[ˈmukka]

αγελάδα

[ajɛˈlaða]

암소

[am.so]

母牛

[mǔˈniú]

بقرة

[ˈbaqara]

פרה

[paˈʁa]

うし

[ɯʃi]

корова

[kɐˈrovə]

Franz Marc, *Cows, Yellow-Red-Green*

hare

[her]

lapin

[lapɛ̃]

liebre

[ˈljeβre]

lepre

[ˈlɛːpre]

λαγός

[laˈɣɔs]

заяц

[ˈzaɪt͡s]

Hase

[ˈhaːzə]

토끼

[tʰo.k'i]

兔子

[tùzi]

أرنب

[ˈʔarnæb]

ארנב

[aʁˈnav]

うさぎ

[ɯsagi]

Albrecht Dürer, *Young Hare*

말
[mal]

马
[mǎ]

حصان
[ħɨˈsˤaːn]

конь
[konʲ]

うま
[ɯma]

סוס
[sus]

Pferd
[pfeːɐ̯t]

horse
[hɔːs]

cheval
[ʃəval]

άλογο
[ˈaloɣɔ]

cavallo
[kaˈvallo]

caballo
[kaˈβaʎo]

Franz Marc, *Blue Horse I*

chat
[ʃa]

cat
[kæt]

gato
['gato]

Katze
['katsə]

gatto
['gatto]

고양이
[ko.jaŋ.i]

γάτα
['ɣata]

猫
[māo]

кошка
['koʂkə]

قطة
['qɪtˤːa]

ねこ
[neko]

חתול
[ħaˈtul]

Franz Marc, *The White Cat*

perro
['peřo]

chien
[ʃjɛ̃]

cane
['kaːne]

dog
[dɒg]

σκύλος
['scilɔs]

Hund
[hʊnt]

собака
[sɐ'bakə]

개
[kɛː]

いぬ
[inɯ]

狗
[gǒu]

כלב
['kelev]

كلب
[kælb]

Cornelius Völker, *Dog, White*

elefante

[eleˈfante]

elefante

[eleˈfaɳte]

ελέφαντας

[ɛˈlɛfandas]

éléphant

[elefɑ̃]

слон

[slon]

elephant

[ˈɛlɪfənt]

ぞう

[dzoː]

Elefant

[eleˈfant]

פיל

[pil]

코끼리

[kʰo.kʼi.ri]

فيل

[fiːl]

大象

[dàxiàng]

Unknown Indian artist, *Two Princes on a Parade Elephant*

τίγρη
['tiɣri]

tigre
['ti:gre]

тигр
['tʲigər]

tigre
['tiɣre]

とら
[toɾa]

tigre
[tigʀ]

טיגריס
['tigʁis]

tiger
['taɪgə]

نمر
['næmir]

Tiger
[ti:gɐ]

老虎
[lǎohǔ]

호랑이
[ho.raŋ.i]

Unknown Korean artist, *Tiger*

птица
['ptʲit͡sə]

とり
[toɾi]

ציפור
[t͡siˈpoʁ]

طير
[tˤiːr]

鸟
[niǎo]

새
[sɛː]

πουλί
[puˈli]

uccello
[utˈtʃɛllo]

pájaro
[ˈpaxaro]

oiseau
[wazo]

bird
[bɜːd]

Vogel
[ˈfoːɡl̩]

Pablo Picasso, *Dove of Peace*

ハチ
[hatʃi]

oca
[ɐˈsa]

צרעה
[t͡siɐˈʃa]

σφήκα
[ˈsfika]

دبور
[dæˈbːuːr]

vespa
[ˈvɛspa]

黄蜂
[huángfēng]

avispa
[aˈβispa]

말벌
[mal.bəl]

guêpe
[gɛp]

Wespe
[ˈvɛspə]

wasp
[wɒsp]

Ma Ch'üan, *Beauty on the Shrub*

תפוח

[taˈpuaħ]

りんご

[ɾingo]

تفاحة

[tuˈfːæːħə]

яблоко

[ˈjabləkə]

苹果

[pínɡguǒ]

μήλο

[ˈmilɔ]

사과

[sa.gwa]

mela

[ˈmeːla]

Apfel

[ˈapfl̩]

manzana

[mãn̪ˈθana]

apple

[ˈæpəl]

pomme

[pɔm]

Justus Juncker, *Still Life with Apple and Insects*

زجاجة
[zuˈd͡ʒæːd͡ʒə]

בקבוק
[bakˈbuk]

瓶子
[píngzǐ]

びん
[bin]

병
[pjəŋ]

бутылка
[buˈtɨlkə]

Flasche
[ˈflaʃə]

μπουκάλι
[buˈkali]

bottle
[ˈbɒtəl]

bottiglia
[botˈtiʎʎa]

bouteille
[butɛj]

botella
[boˈteʎa]

Craigie Aitchison, *Bottle and Berries Montecastelli*

火腿

[huǒtuǐ]

햄

[hɛm]

Schinken

[ˈʃɪŋkn̩]

ham

[hæm]

jambon

[ʒɑ̃bɔ̃]

jamón

[xaˈmõn]

لحم مملح

[læħm muˈmælːæħ]

נקניק

[nakˈnik]

ハム

[hamɯ]

ветчина

[vʲɪtɕɪˈna]

ζαμπόν

[zamˈbɔn]

prosciutto

[proʃˈʃutto]

케이크
[kʰe.i.kʰɨ]

蛋糕
[dàngāo]

Kuchen
[ˈkuːxn̩]

كعك
[kʌʕk]

cake
[keɪk]

עוגה
[ʕuˈga]

gâteau
[gɑto]

ケーキ
[keːki]

pastel
[paṣˈtel]

пирожные
[pʲɪˈroʐnɨɪ]

torta
[ˈtɔrta]

γλυκό
[ɣliˈkɔ]

Gustave Caillebotte, *Cakes*

Kleid
[kl̥aɪ̯t]

ऊ
[ot]

dress
[dres]

裙子
[qúnzi]

robe
[ʁɔb]

فستان
[fusˈtæːn]

vestido
[bes̞ˈtiðo]

שמלה
[simˈla]

vestito
[vesˈtiːto]

ドレス
[doɾesɯ]

φόρεμα
[ˈfɔɾɛma]

платье
[ˈplatʲɪ]

108

Yinka Shonibare, *Dressing Down*

chaussures

[ʃosyʁ]

zapatos

[θaˈpatos]

scarpe

[ˈskarpe]

παπούτσια

[paˈputsia]

shoes

[ʃuːz]

Schuhe

[ˈʃuːə]

鞋子

[xiézi]

حذاء

[ħiˈðæːʔ]

נעליים

[naʕaˈlajim]

туфли

[ˈtuflʲɪ]

くつ

[kɯtsɯ]

신발

[sin.bal]

Francois Boucher, *Portrait of Madame de Pompadour*

doll

[dɒl]

poupée

[pupe]

muñeca

[muˈɲeka]

bambola

[ˈbambola]

κούκλα

[ˈkukla]

кукла

[ˈkuklə]

Puppe

[ˈpʊpə]

인형

[in.hjəŋ]

洋娃娃

[yángwáwa]

دمية

[ˈdumjə]

בובה

[buˈba]

にんぎょう

[ningjoː]

ballon
[balɔ̃]

ball
[bɔːl]

pelota
[peˈlota]

Ball
[bal]

palla
[ˈpalla]

공
[koːŋ]

μπάλα
[ˈbala]

球
[qiú]

мяч
[mʲat͡ɕ]

كرة
[kura]

ボール
[boːɾɯ]

כדור
[kaˈduʁ]

Henri Rousseau, *The Football Players*

רכבת

[ʁaˈkevet]

train

[treɪn]

train

[trɛ̃]

tren

[tren]

قطار

[qɨˈtˤaːr]

기차

[ki.cʰa]

σιδηρόδρομος

[siðiˈrɔðrɔmɔs]

treno

[ˈtrɛːno]

поезд

[ˈpoɪst]

火车

[huǒchē]

れっしゃ

[reʃːa]

Eisenbahn

[ˈaɪznˌbaːn]

Wassily Kandinsky, *Murnau View with Railway and Castle*

barco
['barko]

bateau
[bato]

nave
['naːve]

boat
[boʊt]

πλοίο
['pliɔ]

Schiff
[ʃɪf]

лодка
['lotkə]

배
[pɛ]

ふね
[ɸɯne]

船
[chuán]

אונייה
[oniˈja]

سفينة
[sæˈfiːnə]

Edward Hopper, *The Martha McKeen of Wellfleet*

bicicletta
[bitʃiˈkletta]

bicicleta
[biθiˈkleta]

ποδήλατο
[pɔˈðilatɔ]

vélo
[velo]

велосипед
[vʲɪləsʲɪˈpʲet]

bicycle
[ˈbaɪsɪkəl]

じてんしゃ
[dʒitenʃa]

Fahrrad
[ˈfaːɐ̯ˌʀaːt]

אופניים
[ofaˈnajim]

자전거
[ca.ʄən.gə]

دراجة
[daˈrːaːd͡ʒə]

自行车
[zìxíngchē]

Advertisement for the womens' cycle *Diana* of the company *Dürrkopp*

αυτοκίνητο
[aftɔˈcinitɔ]

automobile
[autoˈmɔːbile]

машина
[mɐˈʂinə]

coche
[ˈkoʧe]

くるま
[kuɾuma]

voiture
[vwatyʀ]

מכונית
[meχoˈnit]

car
[kɑː]

سيّارة
[sæˈjːaːra]

Auto
[ˈaʊ̯to]

汽车
[qìchē]

자동차
[ce.doŋ.cʰa]

Josef R. Witzel, *Audi*

повозка

[pɐˈvoskə]

ばしゃ

[baʃa]

כרכרה

[kiʁkaˈʁa]

حنطور

[ħænˈtˤʊːr]

马车

[mǎchē]

마차

[ma.cʰa]

άμαξα

[ˈamaksa]

carrozza

[karˈrɔttsa]

carroza

[kaˈřoθa]

calèche

[kalɛʃ]

carriage

[ˈkærɪdʒ]

Kutsche

[ˈkʊtʃə]

Henri Rousseau, *Old Man's Juniet Trap*

ひこうき
[hikoːki]

самолет
[səmɐˈlʲɵt]

מטוס
[maˈtos]

αεροπλάνο
[aɛrɔˈplanɔ]

طائرة
[ˈtˤaːʔira]

aeroplano
[aeroˈplaːno]

飞机
[fēijī]

avión
[aβiˈon]

비행기
[pi.həŋ.gi]

avion
[avj�õ]

Flugzeug
[ˈfluːkˌtsɔɪ̯k]

plane
[pleɪn]

Unknown artist, *The Single-Decker ›Antoinette‹ across a City*

나무
[na.mu]

Baum
[baʊ̯m]

树
[shù]

tree
[triː]

شجرة
[ˈʃæd͡ʒara]

arbre
[aʁbʁ]

עץ
[ʕet͡s]

árbol
[ˈarβol]

き
[ki]

albero
[ˈalbero]

дерево
[ˈdʲerʲɪvə]

δέντρο
[ˈðɛndrɔ]

Gustav Klimt, *Apple Tree I*

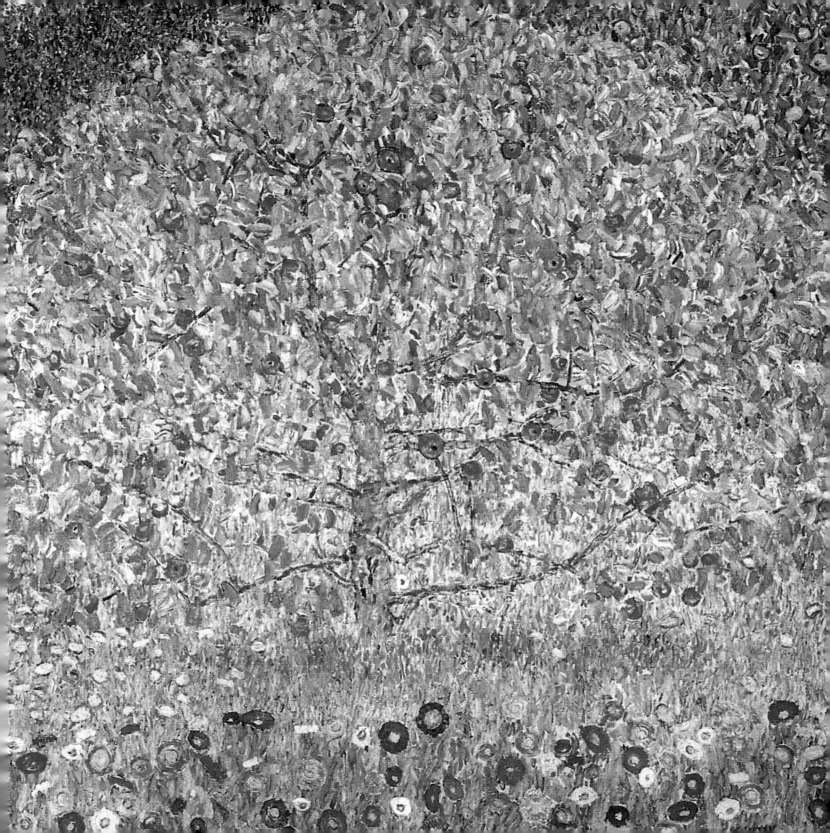

פרחים

[pʁaˈħim]

はな

[hana]

زهور

[zuhuːr]

цветы

[t͡sv ʲɪ ˈtɨ]

花

[huā]

λουλούδια

[luˈluðia]

꽃

[kʼot]

fiori

[ˈfjoːri]

Blumen

[bluːmən]

flores

[ˈflores]

flowers

[ˈflaʊəz]

fleurs

[floeʁ]

130

جِبَال

[d͡ʒiˈbæːl]

山

[shān]

산

[san]

Berge

[ˈbɛʁɡə]

mountains

[ˈmaʊntɪnz]

montagnes

[mõtaɲ]

הָרִים

[haˈʁim]

やま

[jama]

горы

[ˈɡorɨ]

βουνά

[vuˈna]

montagne

[monˈtaɲɲe]

montañas

[mõn̩ˈtaɲas]

Wassili Werestschagin, *Snow-capped Himalaya*

田野

[tiányě]

حقول

[ħuˈquːl]

들

[tɨːl]

שדות

[saˈdot]

Felder

[ˈfɛldɐ]

はたけ

[hatake]

fields

[fiːldz]

поля

[pɐˈlʲæ]

champs

[ʃɑ̃]

χωράφια

[xɔˈrafia]

campos

[ˈkampos]

campi

[ˈkampi]

Grant Wood, *Young Corn*

봄
[pom]

春天
[chūntiān]

Frühling
[ˈfʀyːlɪŋ]

الربيع
[arːaˈbɪːʕ]

spring
[sprɪŋ]

אביב
[aˈviv]

printemps
[pʀɛ̃tɑ̃]

はる
[haɾɯ]

primavera
[primaˈβera]

весна
[vʲɪsˈna]

primavera
[primaˈvɛːra]

άνοιξη
[ˈaniksi]

Utagawa Hiroshige, *The Plum Garden at Kameido*

Sommer

['zɔmɐ]

summer

['sʌmə]

été

[ete]

verano

[beˈrano]

estate

[esˈtaːte]

καλοκαίρι

[kalɔˈcɛri]

여름

[jə.ɾɨm]

夏天

[xiǎtiān]

الصيف

[aˈsˤːajf]

קיץ

['kajit͡s]

なつ

[natsɯ]

лето

['lʲetə]

Georges Seurat, *Bathers at Asnière*

otoño
[oˈtoɲo]

الخريف
[ælxaˈriːf]

automne
[otɔn]

秋天
[qiūtiān]

Herbst
[hɛʁpst]

가을
[ka.il]

autumn/fall
[ˈɔːtəm/faːl]

סתיו
[stav]

autunno
[auˈtunno]

あき
[aki]

φθινόπωρο
[fθiˈnɔpɔrɔ]

осень
[ˈosʲɪnʲ]

Giuseppe Arcimboldo, *Autumn*

winter
['wɪntə]

hiver
[ivɛʁ]

invierno
[ĩm'bjerno]

inverno
[in'vɛrno]

χειμώνας
[çi'mɔnas]

зима
[zʲɪ'ma]

Winter
['vɪntɐ]

겨울
[kjə.ul]

冬天
[dōngtiān]

الشتاء
[æʃːi'tæːʔ]

חורף
['ħoʁef]

ふゆ
[ɸɯjɯ]

Lucas I. van Valckenborch, *Winter Landscape with Snowfall near Antwerp*

glace
[glas]

ice
[aɪs]

hielo
[ˈʤelo]

Eis
[aɪ̯s]

ghiaccio
[ˈgjattʃo]

얼음
[əl.im]

πάγος
[ˈpaɣɔs]

冰
[bīng]

лед
[lʲɵt]

جَلِيد
[d͡ʒaˈliːd]

こおり
[koːɾi]

קֶרַח
[ˈkeʁaħ]

agua
[ˈaɣwa]

eau
[o]

acqua
[ˈakkwa]

water
[ˈwɔːtə]

νερό
[nɛˈrɔ]

Wasser
[ˈvasɐ]

вода
[vɐˈda]

물
[mul]

みず
[midzɯ]

水
[shuǐ]

מים
[ˈmajim]

ماء
[mæːʔ]

fuoco

['fwɔːko]

fuego

['fweɣo]

φωτιά

[fɔ'tça]

feu

[fø]

огонь

[ɐ'gonʲ]

fire

[faɪə]

ひ

[hi]

Feuer

['fɔɪ̯ɐ]

אש

[eʃ]

불

[pul]

نار

[naːr]

火

[huǒ]

Louis Anquetin, *Child and Fireplace*

ήλιος
['iʎɔs]

солнце
['sont͡sə]

たいよう
[taijoː]

שֶׁמֶשׁ
['ʃemeʃ]

شمس
[ʃæms]

太阳
[tàiyáng]

sole
['soːle]

sol
[sol]

soleil
[sɔlɛj]

sun
[sʌn]

Sonne
['zɔnə]

해
[hɛ]

Vincent van Gogh, *The Sower at Sunset*

дождь

[doʂtʲ]

βροχή

[vrɔˈçi]

あめ

[ame]

pioggia

[ˈpiɔddʒa]

גשם

[ˈgeʃem]

lluvia

[ˈʎuβja]

مطر

[ˈmatˤar]

pluie

[plɥi]

雨

[yǔ]

rain

[reɪn]

비

[pi]

Regen

[ˈʀeːgn̩]

Utagawa Hiroshige, *A Sudden Shower over Ohashi and Atake*

くも
[kɯmo]

облака
[əblɐ'ka]

עננים
[ʕana'nim]

σύννεφα
['sinɛfa]

سحاب
[sæˈħæ:b]

nuvole
['nu:vole]

云
[yún]

nubes
['nuβes]

구름
[ku.rɨm]

nuages
[nyaʒ]

Wolken
['vɔlkn̩]

clouds
[klaʊdz]

Eugéne Boudin, *Blue Sky, White Clouds*

ירח
[jaˈʁeaħ]

つき
[tsɯki]

قمر
[ˈqamar]

луна
[lʊˈna]

月亮
[yuèliàng]

φεγγάρι
[fɛŋˈgari]

달
[tal]

luna
[ˈluːna]

Mond
[moːnt]

luna
[ˈluna]

moon
[muːn]

lune
[lyn]

Adam Elsheimer, *The Flight into Egypt*

The words in this book

The pictures in this book

© Prestel Verlag, Munich · London · New York, 2014

© for the works held by the artists or their legal heirs except for: Leonhard Tsuguharu Foujita, Wassily Kandinsky, Roy Lichtenstein, Rahman Yinka Shonibare, Cornelius Völker: © VG Bild-Kunst, Bonn 2014; Pablo Picasso: © Succession Picasso / VG Bild-Kunst, Bonn 2014; Andy Goldsworthy: © Andy Goldsworthy; Salvador Dalí: © Salvador Dalí, Fundació Gala – Salvador Dalí / VG Bild-Kunst, Bonn 2014; Craigie Aitchison und Francks Deceus: © The Bridgeman Art Library, 2014; Edward Hopper: © Colección Carmen Thyssen-Bornemisza en depósito en el Museo Thyssen-Bornemisza / Scala, Florence 2014

Cover: Franz Marc, *Cows, Yellow-Red-Green*

Frontispiece: Alexej von Jawlensky, *The Teddy Bear Family*

P. 5: Seymour Joseph Guy, *Knowledge is Power*

Prestel, a member of Verlagsgruppe Random House GmbH
Prestel Verlag, Munich

Prestel Publishing Ltd.
14-17 Wells Street
London W1T 3PD

Prestel Publishing
900 Broadway, Suite 603
New York, NY 10003

www.prestel.com

Library of Congress Control Number is available; British Library Cataloguing-in-Publication Data: a catalogue record for this book is available from the British Library; Deutsche Nationalbibliothek holds a record of this publication in the Deutsche Nationalbibliografie; detailed bibliographical data can be found under: http://dnb.ddb.de

Prestel books are available worldwide. Please contact your nearest bookseller or one of the above addresses for information concerning your local distributor.

Author: Doris Kutschbach
Translated and copyedited by: zappmedia GmbH
Picture editor: Sabine Tauber
Design: Meike Sellier
Layout: Corinna Pickart
Production: Astrid Wedemeyer
Origination: Reproline Mediateam, Munich
Printing and Binding: TBB, a. s.

Verlagsgruppe Random House FSC® N001967
The FSC®-certified paper *Profibulk* was supplied by Igepa.

ISBN 978-3-7913-7174-0